The Hu Portion

Nicola Warwick

V.

Published in the United Kingdom in 2023
by V. Press,
10 Vernon Grove,
Droitwich,
Worcestershire,
WR9 9LQ.

ISBN: 978-1-7398838-2-9

Cover photo & design © Sarah Leavesley, 2023
Printed in the U. K. on FSC accredited paper by 4edge Limited, www.4edge.co.uk/

Acknowledgements

*'The ninth wave' in 'The Healing' refers to the sailing term of the same name meaning
the very large wave that comes after a series of much smaller ones.*
*Words and phrases in italics in 'Watering with the Angle Shades (Phlogophora
meticulosa)' are taken or adapted from Wikipedia.*
*Thanks are due to the editors of the following magazines where some of these poems
have previously appeared: Acumen, Artemis, Brittle Star, The Frogmore Papers and
Shooter Literary Magazine.*
*'Colony Collapse Syndrome' was awarded first prize in Suffolk Poetry Society's Crabbe
Memorial Poetry Competition in 2021; 'Spring Tide' was commended in the same
competition in 2019.*
*Many thanks are also due to past and present members of the Poetry School's
Wymondham Seminar, led initially by Moniza Alvi and currently by Heidi Williamson.*
Thanks above all to Sarah James at V. Press for bringing this book into the world.

Contents

Colony Collapse Syndrome

After the first month, she stopped paying the bills,
wrapped herself in moth-chewed layers,
shivered in the dark.

She lost colour without heat and light.
The house opened like a cave
ready for what might come in.

Bats roosted in cornices.
Mice and silverfish scuttled over
the bare floor at night.

She netted her hair with spider silk
to keep it out of her eyes, became
a queen of wings and shadows.

At night, fox cubs played on the stairs.
Sometimes, she felt the bristles
of their young snouts.

She set trails of sugar water to draw in
the specialists. Her house filled with bees
who droned serenades,

brought offerings sticky with nectar.
She lay on a mattress on the floor,
allowed them to worship her.

Garden Cross Spiders

When we walked to the hospital, I noticed those spiders,
hanging at regular intervals in the hedgerows.

They were always busy building their disc-like webs,
or just waiting, head down, for something to land.

I liked best the way they could be startled
into life by a puff of my breath, their movement

precise, like swimming – or walking on the moon.
I studied their colours, the lines on their backs,

how they all looked different, and yet the same.
My delaying tactics; I regressed thirty years,

desperate to see one trap a fly or wasp, binding it
for safekeeping in its larder, tight as an invalid –

like my father in his hospital bed, side-rails in place,
though he hadn't shifted on his own for days.

Late high summer

For the first time that season, butterflies appear, flying with such
urgency I can only see their brown underwings. One, at rest
on the path, opens and closes with the pulse of a sleepy heart.

Out walking, I stumble on a nest of bees, a furry black tar spilling
from hard earth. Parched ground aches for water. Cracks stretch
along field edges where hares lie shaded under dry wheat.

Summer birds stage air shows, scything the air. Fledglings test
their wings, land on roofs, aerials, telegraph wires,
calling to each other.

When the day cools, you lead me down the garden,
to the old barn where they were nesting. Our feet whisper
across a lawn more straw than grass.

As our eyes adjust to the dim, we make out a cup of dried mud,
small as a hand, where the young were reared. Now, they are
roosting so close above my head I could pick one like an apple.

Not yet asleep, they are unsettled by our presence
and we slip outside where the sky, red as a swallow's throat,
is raising up the moon.

The Chitterings

Night by night, I listen
for the soft scrape of their claws
as they slip out from under the eaves.

You doze beside me, unaware
of the little interlopers who stir only
as we are readying ourselves for sleep.

I wait for the dusky light to fade,
for their ragged shapes to take to the air,
for them to stutter like ticker-tape into the dark.

My ears are tuned like a child's for their speech,
their squeals and calls, a quiet chit-chittering
as they gather for the off.

You say it's all in my head, these creatures
that will not silence, suggest I still them
with something like mindfulness.

On those nights when sleep won't come,
I watch from the window for their exodus,
count them out, count them all back in.

When I hear your voice

"It was the voice of a human being – a known, loved, well-remembered voice – and it spoke in pain and woe, wildly, eerily, urgently."
Jane Eyre, Charlotte Bronte

I hear your voice in the moorland grasses,
in the branches of the trees that stoop before the wind,

in the twists of roots mired underground, in the deeps
and hollows of this landscape, in the browns and purples

of the heathers, the courses and junctions of the streams
and footpaths that cross-hatch the terrain,

the weather-beaten heights, the gritstone hulks that oversee
the hillsides, in the keen of the hawk scything the air,

in the slink of the fox, dance of the hare, colours of bog rosemary,
dwarf cornel, cloudberry, the ascension of the skylark,

the drawn-out call of the curlew, the heavy-hanging
morning mist, the night sky with its gatherings of stars.

All this in my lungs, my skin and hair, steeped in my clothes,
my blood, fixed by the story that joins us.

Kestrel

O, you are a precious thing –
tiny on the falconer's arm.

In the eye of your prey, you are huge,
dropping from tree to ground

to snare a meal. When you rest,
the sun adores you,

coppers your back,
turns you immortal.

Spring Tide

This can't be the place.

Water is a glossy strip in the distance,
the line between sky and sea.

A tide that has ebbed too far,
doesn't know when to stop:

this wanderer
who might never come back

like the barely-there footprints of children
scuffing the sand,

this participant in salty tantrums,
snatcher of cliffs, masher of houses to driftwood.

I'm on edge, want to call it in,
        reel it back, summon the moon:

come in, come home,
all is forgiven.

All is forgiven.
Come in, come home.

Reel it back, summon the moon.
        I'm on edge, want to call it in:

snatcher of cliffs, masher of houses to driftwood,
this participant in salty tantrums,

scuffing the sand
like the barely-there footprints of children

who might never come back.
This wanderer

doesn't know when to stop,
a tide that has ebbed too far,

the line between sky and sea.
Water is a glossy strip in the distance.

This can't be the place.

The Healing

I count the waves – one, two, three
up to the ninth. Is this what I want?

The sea is doing its best to soothe me
unfolding gently on the shingle –
each wave ends on an outbreath
its surface a little ruffled.

Now and then a small crest
breaks before it reaches land –
a creature not sure when to emerge.

And what the sea leaves behind:
crab claw
cuttlefish bone
gull wing-feather
length of driftwood in the shape of a femur.

The water is sequinned with chinks of the sun.
Where is the ninth wave?

A stone like a heart with its back chipped out
big black bubbles of bladderwrack
chalky layers of fossilised oyster-shell
a cat shark's leathery egg case.

I breathe in salt from the air, its healing minerals:
potassium   calcium   magnesium.
On my skin, my hair, in my mouth tastes of:
durability   loyalty   purification.

My broken pieces are slotting back in place.
I time my breath by the ninth wave.

Casting off

One glance at the sea and you're caught.
Water caresses every depth, each of your contours
an inlet, a bay, a rocky cove
where no boat can find a purchase.

Kelp tickles your tender places.
You are a coastline where the sea rasps
at your flesh like the raw tongue
of a big cat. Step out of yourself.

Shed those weights that keep you grounded.
Be brave and shuck the seven layers
of skin, spread yourself as
a septet in gauze on the sand.

Pile nails and teeth as weird cairns.
Detangle muscle and sinew, unravel nerves
and veins, flaunt the glisten of your lymphatic system
in a fantasy of stacks and towers.

Strip right down to your moon-bleached bones.
Take nothing with you. Leave it all to the sea.

Mammalian Dive Reflex

I dip my hands and they are silver underwater
before I plunge into the rush and shock of cold.

My breathing stops as if I've forgotten
how to do it, then I steady; lungs shallow-fill,

heart fierce in my chest. I dive
and the lake is a new realm below –

a rich underworld of waterweed
and slabs of slate like fallen tombstones.

I swim to the light, my head, back, shoulders
carve the surface again and again like an otter.

Once more, I dive down, down, my hands so numb
they could hold nothing precious.

I am all bones and liquid.
My eyes are round and lucid.

Between my fingers, webs of skin.
My feet fuse to a tail.

How long my breath will hold,
I do not know.

Mirage

Hottest day of the year so far:
the street swells and sighs,
buildings close inwards.
Each brick hot to the touch,
ground cracks open
in this sun-dried, rainless land.

We search the sky for respite,
wanting the first wisp of cloud
to promise storm, but catch only
something drifting, wings
outstretched for a languid flap
as it traces a continuous course.

The heat haze makes it *buzzard*,
vulture. We squint and offer
cormorant in error before it fixes
as a heron, circling, circling,
searching for the wet.

Reedham Staithe

From where we sat on the quay,
it looked like nothing but an old blanket
left useless at a pylon's foot.

It was not till we saw the old man
labouring across the bridge
that we understood.

Who'd have thought a clump of feathers
could hold such weight, could make a man
bend like a crack willow rod?

Its neck safe in his hands, its unclean head
nestled in the hollow of his hip
as he walked, slowly, slowly;

its wings swung open, closed,
then open again against his back,
a landlocked body aching for flight.

Geese at Dusk

They have flown from Svalbard,
those miles small compared
to the reward of fresh feeding grounds:
crops, root vegetables, the tops of beet.
A man with a camera is waiting
for this spectacle to unfold
as it did yesterday, will do
tomorrow, but this day is his.
Beyond the mudflats, he watches,
zoom lens trained for the moment
that he knows will come.
He is waiting for that point when
this wall of monochrome will know
to move, when the air
is charged enough for them to go.
          He is stilled by the sight
of these birds, how they take off
together, long necks extended,
each synchronised with its neighbour
in a rush of wings and calls.
The sky fades like an old bruise.
He cannot contain the girth
of the flock with a camera,
can only watch as they pour
inland to roost, their bellies glazed
with the citrine light of dusk.

Wing, grounded, on the pavement

no elegant fan
this clutch of pigeon-grey feathers
      more like a bird beginning
to shift to something else
to drop its plumage in clumps
as part of an exchange
from avian to human – a bird
discarding part of itself
and leaving a trail that says
      yes, I've been here
watch me go
an Ariel with one wing
hanging from its shoulder
on a thread of skin –
a dead weight
these feathers snipped off
nipped clean from the body
by expert teeth –
      couldn't have got away –
how unbalanced would it be
one wing drooping down
and left only with the memory

She dreams of being this

She thinks first of swans
with curved necks and plumage
like old snow. Then she considers
eagles with hunter's beaks
and far-seeing, topaz eyes.
She thinks all this and sleeps
with feathers under her pillow,
dreams herself a quilt
of reeds.
              She sleeps in dreams
of elegance, of broad wings
and unswerving flight paths.
When she wakes, she is not all this –
her body squat and dark,
her voice grates like an unoiled
engine.
              In the tunes
of the morning, she hears
the birds in limbering song.
She calls and calls, too long –
she calls and her song
rattles like a warning.

January

No one here today but the old man counting
whooper swans, lost in the cloud of birds
that stream across the flat tableau of the Wash.

He's here because there's nowhere else
to go, no one to tell him not to sit on the cold
wooden bench inscribed to the memory of a stranger.

He listens to the music of the season: the chafe
of the wind, layer on layer of bird calls, a cacophony
of goose-song, winter's greys echoed in a rush of flight feathers.

His thoughts are lost in the mudflats, water silvering
in the sun, fields where the remains of last year's harvest
are grazed by pink-footed geese. A curlew's voice cleaves the air.

He watches with the ease of a man whose time is empty,
who listens more than he knows how to speak. An egret stalks
the shallows, a left-over ghost, carrying its egg-tight grief.

17.15 from Wymondham

At first, they could be anything:
horses, large bushes, very big dogs –

one of those not-quite-sure moments –
they're in the corner of a field –
the cusp of it nearest the line,

a group of five, or six, or more,
poised, heads up, staring at my train.

As it pulls closer, I pick out
the bronzy tone of their coats,

their slender necks, ears pricked up
and listening for wolves.

I'm almost eye-to-eye with them.

They're all looking at me;
each one has had a silent signal
from the others

 – look, here it comes,
that thing we don't have a name for –
the noise and speed of it –

all watching it rattle past,
as if they have nothing better to do.

Wild horses

The soft arc of neck, blur of mane against a peaty coat. Shiver of tail. Muscle twitch of flank. Bold flick of head. The steady leg, the turn of a hoof that has not known the blacksmith's hands. Slope of spine like a hill in an ancient vista. The depth of eye, looking right back from the past. Catch the stories they hold.

Their gait, the fluid drive across all terrains. Catch them motionless as mounds on a barren moorland, these all-weather breeds, their smell of autumn, of woodland. Catch them as engineers of landscape, the heart of them, how they shape fenland, grassland, wetland with their trampling, wallowing, cropping of unwanted scrub.

Catch them on tor and fell, heath and dale: Exmoor, New Forest, Tarpan, Konik, Cob, Eriskay. Stallions glowering like storm clouds on hillsides. Harems of mares and their young grazing on herbs and coarse grass. Catch them in harsh places where people will not live. Catch them skittish and nervous of humans.

Catch them in dirt, red ochre, animal blood, with the end of a brush made from twig. Catch them in red, yellow, black, coloured into life. Catch the core that keeps them half-wild.

The huff of charcoal
brushing paper, uncertain
outbreath of greeting.

Hare, in the garden

Mornings, you stretch your long, lean limbs,
unhunch your shoulders, unleash
those streamered ears to the sun.

You are all legs I wouldn't know what to do with.
My hand aches for the round of your back,
your coat the colour of last season's bracken.

You are more used to hunkering down
than drawing attention to yourself.

You throw me a look.
You're tense and ready to run.

I watch from the patio as you lope
across the lawn, dip your head
to breakfast on grass and moss.

Your whole self is daytime and energy.
Your coat fleckles in the morning light.

Those citrine eyes miss nothing.

If I get too close, you rise up
on those never-ending legs,
ghost yourself away.

And the trees (said)

In the shiver of leaves
I heard silence.

In the creak of a heavy bough
I heard calm.

In the down-flight of seed-pods
I heard the soothing of words

twisting
          ground-wards.

In the shimmer of birdsong
I heard the shameless laughter of children.

In the whisper of bark unpeeling
I heard the tearing of scorn.

When rain fell on the sun-scorched greenery
it was the long, sated sigh of a lover.

And roots easing through earth
were a voice making itself unheard.

Watering with the Angle Shades (Phlogophora meticulosa)

One of those evenings. Sky the colour of apricots. Bees sleeping in the lavender. No sign yet of the Corn Moon. The ground firm from lack of rain. Shadows elongate across the lawn. I am drunk on night-scented stock. Grass whispers under my bare feet. I wander the garden, water the plants.

Something dark rises from the strawberry patch. Settles on the path. Shivers brown, wet wings. I lean down. Soon, on my hand, an inch-long moth, a stunner in quiet colours.

Common name – owlet. Of the Noctuidae family. First described by Linnaeus in 1758. Mainly flies at night. Found throughout Europe. Strongly migratory. Forewings shaped with sharply pointed apex. Base colour buffish brown. Marked with a bold 'V' in pink and green. May be seen during the day on fences and garden foliage. Attracted to light and sugar. Wears disruptive patterning camouflage.

I hang it in the pear tree, a tawny chip against the green. Watch as it waits there, passing for withered fruit.

Recorded food plants include: celery pear dead nettle strawberry red valerian oak birch ivy lettuce hop tobacco bramble dock spinach grape mint sunflower dahlia apple geranium

I leave it to itself, refill my watering can. Mimic a downpour. Drench the late-summer veg.

The Telling

How to speak of this
          clearing the land of grass/crops
shifting rocks/stones   sieving the earth
mapping the plot with string and stakes

How to speak of this
          the delicacy of uncovering   sweeping the soil/clay clear of
the grave
each bone time-stained/soiled
fragile as eggshell

The naming of bones radius ulna femur
          defleshed
measuring the weight/girth/length
each name new on the tongue

searching each limb/each rib for disease
              each vertebra for signs of degeneration
the giveaway pits and pock-marks

How to speak of
the mound of a skull   crowning the surface/a weird birth
of grave goods   buckles   a knife
the shaft of a sword blade greened with age

How to speak of the whisper/skim of trowel and brush
hands aching for each nub of bone   the honeycomb maze of marrow
          teeth the colour of ivory
a coin in the mouth

How to speak of this
          remains shielded from the elements/the zing of cold air
each brushstroke the exhale of a long-held breath

How to speak of this
          the labour/ the toil releasing each part
pulse by pulse from the mud

The Courteous Farmer

Beltane, and the first morning for a while
this early riser hasn't woken with the aches and pains
of age. As normal, he is abroad, striding the fields,
lost in how summer mist softens his landscape.

He roams the lanes too, scouring the edges
for roadkill, something tasty for the pot,
to save the missus a trip to town for fresh meat.

Then, centred in the track, he spots
the tawny outline of a hare, head mashed-in,
bulging eyes split open. Her long limbs
remind him of the children they will not have.

Drawing near, he spies movement in the swell
of her belly, a tiny life trying to escape.
Turning butcher, he cleaves her open,

pulls out the bedraggled body of her young,
its eyes still closed, fur wet with birth matter.
He wraps it tight in the deep of his jacket,
ignores the bloody stain against his shirt,

takes it home, a new pet for his wife.
By the fire, he feeds it colostrum from his cattle,
holds it to his chest, a second heart.

Husk

It's big as a child's globe,
and light as a balloon
filled with nothing
but empty parlours.

I unhook it
from the ceiling of this tiny
wooden hut.

To crush it like an eggshell
would be reckless.

Its outer layer starts
to flake at my touch,
leaves a dusty lining
on my fingers.

With my late father's penknife
I start to cut, slowly,
a gentle sawing motion.

The layers give
like a body not exposed
for a thousand years.

All I'm doing is wrecking
the long-abandoned chambers
where phrases used to hide.

And at the heart, nothing –
no sign of drones or the queen
who chewed wood pulp
with saliva.

Some layers are the petals
of a brilliant dead flower,

others the husk of a fruit
that won't give up its meat.

I know this is not something
I can reassemble.

The whole is a barren cave
that once held something
I can no longer name.

How he keeps her

He was in awe of her skin,
the way its colour shifted in the light,
vanished beneath her clothes
as if she were not flesh but water underneath.

And how her hair shivered around her face,
the long strands clutching at his eyes,
his mouth, even on days when the air
was at its calmest.

There must have been fluid in her bones,
the way her body flexed and bent as he held her,
his rough, working hands grabbing
at the still, smooth, almost-not-there of her.

He tasted salt on her lips, in the water
that pooled in her eyes when she spoke,
when she gazed at the vast bulk of the sea,
and sobbed at the retreating tide.

There was a keening in her voice
as he walked back from the beach,
a limp, dark pelt across his arm,
as he tossed it on the fire,

as it fought and writhed,
over and over on itself.

Harbour Spell

On days when the glitter of sand
is not enough, nor the glamour
of shells,
        what can I do?

Can I ask for saltwater
silvered by the moon,
or rumpled by a wind
that does not know its own strength?

My eyes are wet and canine.
My ears spiral into whelk
and slipper limpet, strain
for that one song.
        My lips are saline.

How long can I breathe underwater?
How many stones should I stash
in my pockets?
How long will it take for the water's
grip to ripen me to sealskin?

You and the sea and a prayer

To dive is an act of worship –
just you and the sea –
breathe in, out,
take in the crystal blue
of this lucid third dimension.

Just you and the sea –
your breath bubbles out
into this other world
where all creatures
are wonders in bold colours.

You and the sea and mythology –
leave a piece of yourself
in this underworld
as a promise you will come back.

You and the sea and the silence –
each dive is vital as prayer,
each breath a little sacrifice.

The Fijian Mermaid

He said he'd show me mermaids and I wanted
silver scales and long hair that floated like jetsam
on the water. I wanted pearls round their necks,
combs of shells, mirrors of dazzled glass,
a tail of both muscle and light.
I wanted a half-woman with a body full as milk,
a face to make a sailor dive for, the bulk of a manatee,
the weight of her held by the brine as she played peek-a-boo
in the mangroves. Or a grey, sleek thing, lifting her face to the sky,
crooning to watchers on the shore, slipping off her skin,
hiding it behind rocks while she danced in her wet skirts
with a human lover.
                                    But I got this – a hybrid
of wrinkles, dried and stretched like a thing past
its best, too long out of water and held back
from another age, skinny arms clamped over its ears,
mouth frozen in a scream. Something like a mummy
stitched together as a patchwork, not a thing
of wonder, more a relic yearning
to be laid to rest, craving its human portion.

Lighthouse

The flame shivers as a breeze
coaxes its way into the room.

Dusk has come; you have not noticed
the light fail, the sky soften

to a chilly blue. Dark birds cross
the garden, sink into the trees

to roost, call to each other
in shades of melancholy.

A few minutes more – your eyes
ache at the view, scour

the expanse of sky for one speck
of light, small warmth

of a yellow planet piercing the cold,
flickering like a spark that yearns to ignite.

Nothing more for you to do here.
You clear your throat, blow out the candle –

let the dust settle.

NICOLA WARWICK lives in Suffolk and works in local government. She is a member of Second Light and the Suffolk Poetry Society, whose Crabbe Memorial Poetry Competition she won in 2021. Her work has appeared in various anthologies and magazines, including *Agenda*, *Acumen*, *Mslexia* and *South*. Twice longlisted in the National Poetry Competition and shortlisted for the Bridport Prize, her work embraces the natural world, folklore and relationships, sometimes in combination. Her V. Press pamphlet, *The Human Portion*, follows her previous one, *Naming the Land* (Maytree Press), inspired by her home county. She can be found on Twitter as @warwick_nicola.